Finding
Bethlehem
in the Midst of
Bedlam

Finding
Bethlehem
in the Midst of
Bedlam

by James W. Moore

DVD Study

Leader Guide
BY JOSEPH CROWE

Abingdon Press / Nashville

Contents

Introduction:
How to
Lead This Study

Finding Bethlehem in the Midst of Bedlam is a small-group study about how Christ breaks through our confusion to bring us the peace and love of Christmas. There are five sessions in this study, including one for each week of Advent and one for Christmas. (For more information about the meaning and symbolism behind Advent and Christmas, and their relationship to each other, visit *www.umc.org/what-we-believe/what-is-advent*.)

For this study, in addition to this leader guide you will need the accompanying DVD, as well as the book *Finding Bethlehem in the Midst of Bedlam: An Advent Study for Adults*, by James W. Moore. While this group study will include discussion and activities related to the video clips you will see on the DVD, it will also draw upon content from the book. As the leader, you will want to read the book carefully in advance, make notes and highlight important topics, and familiarize yourself with each chapter. It is highly recommended that each participant in your small group have a copy of the book as well, and that group members spend time on their own reading and reflecting upon the content before the group meeting. This will enable better participation and will provide your group with a deeper, more beneficial experience of the study. Daily devotionals are included in each chapter of the book to guide personal reading throughout the week.

If you have limited experience leading a small group, don't worry. This study is designed to take you and your group through each session in an easy-to-follow way. Think of yourself more as a facilitator and a guide for your group, as you will also be a participant along the journey. Taking time to prepare for each session in advance will help you to be more comfortable in your role as the group's guide.

Below are some of the things you will want to think about and prepare for in advance of your group's meeting each week.

Meeting Space

Arrange for a space that can comfortably accommodate all of the members of your group. Each week, make sure there are a sufficient number of comfortable seats, good lighting, and an outside noise-level that won't make group discussion difficult. If you will be meeting in a room at church or some other public facility, be certain to reserve the room in advance for the particular days and times you will need it. You may also want to decorate your meeting space with an Advent wreath or Christmas decorations. (For more information about the symbolism of the Advent wreath, visit *www.umc.org/what-we-believe/what-do-the-candles-in-our-advent-wreath-mean*.)

Supplies

Make sure each week that you have access to a television and a DVD player that are in good working order, as well as an adequate power source for them. If you know you will be doing an activity for which you'd like to have participants find information online, make sure your meeting space has accessible Internet connectivity, and check it in advance. During the time your group members are arriving and greeting one another, you may want to play some quiet, thoughtful music on a CD or on a handheld device, to set a tone for peacefulness, reflection, and immersion into God's message. You will want to have a number of Bibles on hand each week, as well as pens or pencils and paper. You can remind participants to bring their own personal Bibles if they choose. Look over the session plan in advance each week to see what additional supplies you may need.

Scripture

Each week, carefully read the key Scripture verses that are provided for that week's session. Think about how each verse relates to the subject of that week's theme. You may find online Bible commentaries to help you dig deeper into the context and the background behind the Scripture readings. Your pastor may have suggestions for other commentaries and Bible study helps.

Group Discussion and Activities

Invite and encourage active participation and discussion from all group members. Let them know at your first meeting that you want everyone to work together to create an environment of trust and respect in your group. This will help set everyone at ease about sharing personal reflections and memories, responding to questions, asking questions of their own, and listening to others' thoughts and ideas. Be sensitive to the fact that some people are more comfortable than others opening up in a group setting, and remind yourself that this is all right. The idea is not to force people to move beyond their comfort zones, but to set a tone where people feel welcomed and will enjoy sharing and being involved. As the group facilitator, set the tone by listening carefully to each person's answers and comments, asking follow-up questions of your own, or asking someone to say more when you sense that additional insight or understanding would be helpful.

The order of the discussions, video clips, and activities may vary a bit from one session to the next, so be sure to keep that in mind as you prepare each week. Ultimately, however, the decision is yours as to what each session will include. As you look over the material for each week's meeting, try to estimate generously the amount of time you think you may need for each part of the discussion, for watching the video clips, for doing the activities, and so on. While you will want to keep an eye on the time allotted for your weekly meeting in order to ensure good use of it, remember also to remain flexible and open to going "off-script" sometimes. Your group's experience of the material will be unique to you and to the members of your group, so leave room for God to guide you in different directions.

In addition to group discussions, think about other ways to get your group members invested and involved in every session. Ask for others' help in making sure you have an adequate space in which to meet every week; in getting the equipment and supplies you will need; in reading key Scripture verses, passages from the book, or prayers; in providing refreshments if you choose; or in sharing a special story, song, or conversation piece that relates to the week's material. And remember every week to let your fellow participants know how much you appreciate them and their presence.

Session 1:
Bethlehem or Bedlam

Key Scripture: Luke 2:8-14

Overview

This session explores how the peace and serenity Christ brings can be found even in the midst of chaos and disquiet, and it gives us the keys to finding Bethlehem—that is, the real spirit and meaning of Christmas—in the course of our sometimes hectic lives.

Learning Focus:
- discovering who God is and what God is like
- discovering how to relate to other people
- discovering what really matters

Prepare

As a reminder, review the sections in How to Lead This Study regarding Meeting Space and Supplies. Read pages 7 through 40 of the book *Finding Bethlehem in the Midst of Bedlam*, by James W. Moore; read over the key Scripture for this week; watch the DVD clip for Week 1 in advance; and make notes regarding topics or questions you may want to address with your group. Be sure that you have paper, pens or pencils, posterboard, markers, and Bibles, which you and your group members may need for this week's activities, as well as welcoming music if you wish.

Welcome and Opening Prayer

As group members gather and greet one another, make a point to say hello to each one personally, and give everyone a few minutes to chat and to get settled. When you are ready to begin, thank everyone for coming, and remind them of the topic that you will focus on in today's meeting. Read or summarize the session Overview, and briefly highlight the points of your Learning Focus for today. Lead the group in the opening prayer printed below, or substitute your own.

Opening Prayer

[READ] Dear Lord, it's Christmastime again, or it soon will be, and to be completely honest, there are mixed feelings that come with this. Every year it seems that there's so much to do, so many things to check off the list, so many important details to remember. By the time we get it all done, Christmas is here and gone, and we haven't had—or haven't taken—the time just to breathe, to relax, to reflect, to feel, to be thankful, and to talk with you. It's not clear how much of that is avoidable or changeable, but we need things to be different this year. We need to be able to tune out or get beyond some of the craziness and confusion this time of year can bring. We need to be able to focus on you. We need the inner quiet that only you can provide. We need the peace that comes from the gift you gave to us in the birth of your Son, in the midst of a world of noise and chaos, and from knowing that in him, you set us free. Please let this be our focus and our comfort this Advent season, Dear Lord. Amen.

Open the Session

[READ] Bedlam probably means different things to different people. In your own words, give a definition for bedlam. What are some of the particular characteristics of bedlam in your life—what does it look, sound, and feel like for you? How do you typically deal with bedlam, or do you avoid dealing with it?

Watch the DVD clip for Week 1 entitled "Bethlehem or Bedlam."

[ASK] Where do you see bedlam around Christmastime? What is the source of it, in your experience?

Engage

Read the Scripture and Discuss

Read the following Scripture passage, or ask a volunteer to read it aloud:

Nearby shepherds were living in the fields, guarding their sheep at night. The Lord's angel stood before them, the Lord's glory shone around them, and they were terrified.
The angel said, "Don't be afraid! Look! I bring good news to you—wonderful, joyous news for all people. Your savior is born today in David's city. He is Christ the Lord. This is a sign for you: you will find a newborn baby wrapped snugly and lying in a manger." Suddenly a great assembly of the heavenly forces was with the angel praising God. They said, "Glory to God in heaven, and on earth peace among those whom he favors."

(Luke 2:8-14)

[ASK] Why do you think God chose shepherds to be the first to hear the angels' good news of the Christ Child's birth? Is there anything significant about their profession that equipped them to be the first to hear? Explain your answer.

Activity 1: "Looking for 1 as We Did for 100"

[READ] The DVD clip highlighted modern shepherds at Christmas. Imagine yourself as a shepherd, tending your flock. Think about the shepherd's comment, "If one's missing, we'll . . . spend as much time looking for one as we did for a hundred." Think for a moment about Jesus as the Good Shepherd and yourself as a member of his flock. How does it feel to know that Jesus cares that much for you—that he would drop everything else to find you and bring you home safely if you were lost? Now imagine yourself as the shepherd once more, however this time your flock is made up not of sheep, but of people. If a person were lost, what would you do or say to let him or her know you care the way Jesus cares for you? Write down your thoughts or feelings.

Questions for Group Discussion and Personal Reflection

1. Who in your life has taught you something important or special about the meaning of Christmas? What was special to you about that person, and what did you learn?

2. What gives you a sense of calm and peace when you feel unsettled, nervous, or afraid? Do you have a certain routine that usually works for you in such situations, or do you tend to "wing it" and hope?

3. What would give you a greater sense of control in dealing with the bedlam in your life? When it comes to asking God to take control, do you find it easy or difficult to do, and why? What does asking God to take control require?

4. Try to recall some of your earliest thoughts and ideas about who God is and what God is like. How did these notions shape your faith and your image of God as you grew? How does Jesus' birth in Bethlehem "clear the picture" and change our views about what God is like?

5. What does God's gift to us of his Son Jesus show us about selflessness? How does God's gift to us affect how we relate to other people (or how should it affect us)? Think about a time when someone's act of selflessness moved and inspired you. What did you learn from it?

6. James W. Moore tells us, "We find Bethlehem when we discover what really matters" (*Finding Bethlehem in the Midst of Bedlam*, page 16). How does the Christmas season bring your priorities into focus regarding what really matters?

Activity 2: The Sheep Pen

Give participants paper and pens or pencils. Ask them to draw a simple square or rectangle on half of their sheet of paper to represent a sheep pen. Then, outside the sheep pen, ask group members to draw or write down things that represent bedlam or chaos for them (for example, war or crime). Next, inside the sheep pen, ask group members to draw or write down things that represent their "sheep"—things they'd like to protect and preserve (for example, loved ones, hope, or faith). Then together as a group, share some of the examples group members have come up with, and discuss the following question:

"As 'shepherds,' how might we protect those whom we love and the things that are important to us, when we know we can't enclose them in an actual pen in the real world?"

Activity 3: Breaking Through the Bedlam

As a group, make a "Breaking Through the Bedlam" list of three things that contribute to the feeling of bedlam for you during the season of Advent and Christmas. List specific things that you can resolve to let go of and avoid doing this year, in an effort not to eliminate all the bedlam in your lives, but rather to reduce it. Brainstorm ideas and examples together as a group, but try to reach a consensus on which three items will make up your "official" group list. (If agreement comes easily for your group and three things to let go of seem too few, then make it five things. If you are having difficulty reaching any kind of consensus, then concentrate on listing just one thing.)

Resolve together as a group that each member, including you, will let go of or avoid doing these particular chaos-causing things this season. Then, let participants take a few moments individually to decide on one thing each they'd like to make room for in place of the bedlam-causing things they plan to eliminate. Share these examples with one another. To help keep yourselves accountable, ask the group members to write down on small slips of paper what they will be letting go of and what they plan to add instead. Ask each person to keep his or her slip of paper somewhere close, where he or she will see it daily during this Advent season as a reminder.

Close the Session

Focus for the Week

[READ] As James W. Moore tells us, "Every now and then, we find Bethlehem . . . the real spirit, the real meaning of Christmas" that breaks through the bedlam and keeps us going (*Finding Bethlehem in the Midst of Bedlam*, page 12). For him, it was hearing a child's simple prayer in Bethlehem itself, right in the middle of the city's chaos. Today and each day this week, focus on looking for those kinds of every-now-and-then moments around you. At the same time, look for ways you can bring that kind of a moment to someone else. Spend time in prayer with God each day, asking God to give you the calm, the quietness, and the inspiration you need to open yourself up to God's holy presence and to make way in your heart and mind for the coming of the Christ Child.

Closing Prayer

[READ] Lord, we may not be able to completely eliminate the bedlam in our lives, but we are so grateful to you for showing us that we don't bear the burden of doing that. Thank you for breaking through the bedlam, for meeting us where we are, and for showing us that

Bethlehem and bedlam have always gone together. Help us to look for those every-now-and-then moments that keep us going, and help us to make those moments for others. We thank you for this time together to fellowship, to share, to learn, and to grow closer to you. May we be a blessing to others and may we show them, through the way we live, the peace and love you have shown to us. Amen.

Session 2:
Christ Came to
Set Us Free

Key Scriptures: Galatians 5:13-15; Luke 13:10-17

Overview

This session focuses on how Christ came to set us free from every prison, and how he sends us out into the world as his instruments of compassion, love, and peace to minister to all who are in need.

Learning Focus:
- understanding that Christ frees us from the prison of selfishness
- understanding that Christ frees us from the prison of hate
- understanding that Christ frees us from the prison of unconcern

Prepare

As a reminder, review the sections in How to Lead This Study regarding Meeting Space and Supplies. Read pages 41 through 70 of the book *Finding Bethlehem in the Midst of Bedlam*, by James W. Moore; read over the key Scriptures for this week; watch the DVD clip for Week 2 in advance; and make notes regarding topics or questions you may want to address with your group. Be sure that you have paper, pens or pencils, posterboard, markers, Scotch tape or masking tape, art supplies, multicolor paper, other craft items, and Bibles, which you and your group members may need for this week's activities, as well as welcoming music if you wish.

NOTE: For Activity 1, you may need several current magazines, newspapers, and scissors. See the description for Activity 1, below. For activity 2, you will need craft items specifically suited to constructing handmade Christmas cards. You may also want to be in touch with Rev. John Fanestil in advance about where to send the cards. See the description for Activity 2 below.

Welcome and Opening Prayer

As group members gather and greet one another, make a point to say hello to each one personally, and give everyone a few minutes to chat and to get settled. When you are ready to begin, thank everyone for coming, and remind them of the topic you will focus on in today's meeting. Read or summarize the session Overview, and briefly highlight the points of your Learning Focus for today. Lead the group in the opening prayer printed below, or substitute your own.

Opening Prayer

[READ] Dear Lord, it feels at times like there are so many things in this world that bind us—that tie our hands, close us in, rob us of our senses, and hold us back from being what you want us to be. Help us to understand that life doesn't have to be that way. Help us to see and believe that you have already broken the lock and thrown open the prison doors. Help us to respond to that gift by breaking down the walls that keep people apart and keep them from knowing and loving you. Amen.

Open the Session

[READ] *Freedom* can mean different things to different people. Think for a moment about what you believe it means. Then, in your own words, share your personal definition of *freedom*.

After group members have shared, ask: Among the various definitions given from our group, what commonalities were there? What differences stood out?

Engage

Read the Scripture and Discuss

Read the following Scripture passage, or ask a volunteer to read it aloud:

You were called to freedom, brothers and sisters; only don't let this freedom be an opportunity to indulge your selfish impulses, but serve each other through love. All the Law has been fulfilled in a single statement: *Love your neighbor as yourself.* But if you bite and devour each other, be careful that you don't get eaten up by each other!

(Galatians 5:13-15)

[ASK] What is the apostle Paul saying to us in this passage about the relationship between our personal freedom, selfishness, and the way we treat other people? Why do you think it was so important to Jesus that his way of faith be experienced in community with others, rather than as something we can do entirely on our own? What challenges and opportunities does this present to us?

Watch the DVD clip for Week 2 entitled "Christ Came to Set Us Free."

Questions for Group Discussion and Personal Reflection

In the Parable of the Locksmith, the prisoners are mistaken about their past and current conditions. One of the things this parable shows us is that people can be completely wrong about what they believe to be true. As Christians, how do we walk the path between being confident about serving God's purpose, and being open to the reality that when it comes to some things, we may be in the dark and very wrong in our thinking? How do we balance doing the most good we can with doing the least harm? Is that even the right way to think about how we practice our faith? Why or why not?

1. What does this parable tell us about free will? About denial?

2. After the locksmith has died, how do his followers respond, and what happens to them? What does this illustrate for us about the Christian faith?

3. James W. Moore tells us, "Everywhere we look, people are still in prison" (*Finding Bethlehem in the Midst of Bedlam*, page 43). What does that statement mean to you? What are the realities around us that show this to be true?

4. What does it mean that Jesus "calls us to be not just human but humane" (page 43)? What does it mean to you that Jesus "saves us not just *from* something but also *for* something" (pages 43–44)?

5. How do you respond to the contrast between Christ the Comforter and Christ the Troublemaker? In what ways can Christ be both to each of us?

Activity 1: "Love Conquers" Collage

Take a large piece of posterboard and tape it to a wall. Then, about three or four inches from the bottom of the poster, draw a horizontal line from the left edge to the right. Under the line, write the word *hate* in lowercase letters in the middle of the poster. To the left of the word *hate* write the word *selfishness*, also in lowercase letters. To the right of the word *hate*, write the word *unconcern*.

Next, distribute several current magazines and newspapers, along with pairs of scissors, to the group members. Or ask group members to use their phones or other devices to look for information online—for example, in news headlines. Find several real-world examples of love winning out over hate, selfishness, or unconcern. Be as creative as possible in finding such examples. Briefly describe the examples you have found. Then tape the items you've cut out onto the posterboard in the space above the words *selfishness*, *hate*, and *unconcern*, making a collage. (If your examples come from online, then describe each one in a word or a phrase, and write those down above the line on the posterboard, forming a word collage.) If possible, keep your "Love Conquers" collage hanging on the wall in your meeting space, as a reminder in the coming weeks while you continue your study.

Activity 2: Las Posadas, "The Shelter": Standing with Families Who Are Torn Apart

[READ] In the video clip, we saw families who have been torn apart by US immigration policies, examples of their suffering, and one ministry's efforts to help families on both sides of the US-Mexico border reach through the barriers and celebrate Christmas together. There are complex, challenging problems involved, as all sides acknowledge. In the clip, different church officials affirm that as Christians, we are called to stand for justice and in solidarity with families who are suffering. (For The United Methodist Church's official position on "US Immigration and Family Unity" from *The Book of Resolutions of The United Methodist Church, 2012,* visit *www.umc.org/what-we-believe/us-immigration-and-family-unity.*)

As a group, look up and read the words of Luke 13:10-17. Then discuss the following questions:

1. What do these verses say to us about coming to the assistance of those who are in need and who are suffering?

2. What do they tell us, if anything, about where politics and/or the law fit in with our obligations and our calling as Christians?

3. What is the difference between someone in need right in front of you and someone in need far away? Is there a difference in how we are called to respond as Christians?

4. As Christians, how far do our responsibilities to act on behalf of others go? What role do local, state, and national laws play in how we fulfill these responsibilities?

5. How does helping those who are desperate and in need make the idea of freedom more of a reality to us?

Using art supplies, multicolor paper, markers, pens and pencils, and other craft items, create handmade Christmas cards to send in support of Las Posadas, to be given to families who are separated at Christmas. Use your creativity and your compassion to make cards with messages of encouragement, hope, support, peace, understanding, and Christ's love. Collect the cards you have made, and contact the Reverend John Fanestil at jfanestil@fumcsd.org for information about where to send the cards, and to ask about other ways your small group can be supportive and make a positive difference in the lives of families.

Activity 3: Mission Statement

[READ] Most civic and charitable organizations, as well as most corporations and businesses, have mission statements. For instance, the official mission of The United Methodist Church is "to make disciples of Jesus Christ for the transformation of the world" (see ¶120 of *The Book of Discipline of The United Methodist Church, 2012*, or visit *www.umc.org/what-we-believe/section-1-the-churches*). If it is thoughtfully crafted and communicates its objectives clearly, a mission statement can help you match your values to your actions, and it can guide you in your daily living.

Work together to craft a mission statement for your group. Write it down on posterboard and display it each week. Give careful and creative thought as to what you want to include and how you want it to read. How will your group's mission statement align with and support Jesus' mission? Work together to ensure that it will serve to guide you and inspire you to action.

Close the Session

Focus for the Week

[READ] James W. Moore reminds us that Jesus has opened the doors of our prisons, but Jesus leaves it up to us to decide to walk through the open doors. Jesus "saves us not just *from* something but also *for* something" (*Finding Bethlehem in the Midst of Bedlam*, pages 43-44). As Christians, our responsibility is to take action, to be servants to others, and to do so with Christ's love in our hearts. Read the prayer of Saint Francis of Assisi (*Finding Bethlehem in the Midst of Bedlam*, page 46). Each day this week, pray this prayer to yourself, asking the Lord to make you an instrument of his peace. Reflect upon each line, asking God to show you where there is hatred and how you may sow love there; where there is despair, and how you may sow hope there; and so on. Use this prayer to help you connect your values with your actions.

Closing Prayer

[READ] Dear Lord, thank you for breaking the locks to the prisons that hold us captive and for throwing open the doors. Help us make the decision to walk through those doors and to go out into the world, where you have called us to serve. Show us the ways and the places in which you want us to share your healing love with others, that we may help to bring them restoration and wholeness, as you brought those to us. Amen.

Session 3:
Love Came Down in Bethlehem

Key Scriptures: Matthew 11:1-6; John 3:16-17; Psalm 33

Overview

This session looks at the power of love, and how the love of God born in the Christ Child in Bethlehem is different from all other kinds love.

Learning Focus:
- understanding that love is more powerful than fame
- understanding that love is more powerful than force
- understanding that love is more powerful than money

Prepare

As a reminder, review the sections in How to Lead This Study regarding Meeting Space and Supplies. Read pages 71 through 102 of the book *Finding Bethlehem in the Midst of Bedlam*, by James W. Moore; read over the key Scriptures for this week; watch the DVD clip for Week 3 in advance; and make notes regarding topics or questions you may want to address with your group. Be sure that you have paper, pens or pencils, posterboard, markers, envelopes, and Bibles, which you and your group members may need for this week's activities, as well as welcoming music if you wish.

Welcome and Opening Prayer

As group members gather and greet one another, make a point to say hello to each one personally, and give everyone a few minutes to chat and to get settled. When you are ready to begin, thank everyone for coming, and remind them of the topic you will focus on in today's meeting. Read or summarize the session Overview, and briefly highlight the points of your Learning Focus for today. Lead the group in the opening prayer printed below, or substitute your own.

Opening Prayer

[READ] Dear Lord, you have shown us that love conquers hate, and you have told us that we are to go out into the world and love others. Now, we ask that you help us gain a greater understanding of what love really is—its true power, and how it comes from you. Thank you for the gift of your son, Jesus, who chose the way of love. We pray that you will teach us to love the way Jesus did. Amen.

Open the Session

[READ] Pierre Teilhard de Chardin (1881–1955), a French philosopher and Jesuit priest, is credited with the following the quotation: "Someday, after mastering the winds, the waves, the tides and gravity, we shall harness for God the energies of love, and then, for a second time in the history of the world, man will have discovered fire." What do those words mean, and how do they inspire or challenge you?

Engage

Read the Scripture and Discuss

Read the following Scripture passage, or ask a volunteer to read it aloud:

When Jesus finished teaching his twelve disciples, he went on from there to teach and preach in their cities.
Now when John heard in prison about the things the Christ was doing, he sent word by his disciples to Jesus, asking, "Are you the one who is to come, or should we look for another?"
Jesus responded, "Go, report to John what you

hear and see. Those who were blind are able to see. Those who were crippled are walking. People with skin diseases are cleansed. Those who were deaf now hear. Those who were dead are raised up. The poor have good news proclaimed to them. Happy are those who don't stumble and fall because of me.

(Matthew 11:1-6)

[ASK] How was John the Baptist mistaken about what he believed Jesus' purpose to be? Jesus' reply back to John seems a bit cryptic. What does the manner in which he answered John tell us about Jesus and his purpose?

Activity 1: Love Letter

[READ] Have you ever written a love letter? Perhaps you have, but it's been a long time. Think about someone close to you whom you dearly love (or perhaps more than one person). What is it about this person that makes you love him or her the way you do? What characteristics or qualities does he or she have? What feelings or emotions does he or she stir within you?

Write a letter to that person, expressing your love for him or her. Your letter doesn't have to be long or eloquent. Simply try to say what you feel and why you love him or her the way you do. When you've finished writing, if you wish to share something about your letter with the group, you may do so. If you wish to keep your letter's contents private, just put it into an envelope and take it with you when you leave. If you choose, give your letter to the person(s) who inspired you to write it; or put your letter away as a keepsake and express your love for that special person in another way or when you feel ready to do so.

Watch the DVD clip for Week 3 entitled "Love Came Down in Bethlehem."

Questions for Group Discussion and Personal Reflection

1. What gives a person power in our world today? Recall answers from the DVD, along with others you might add.

2. What sorts of things accompany power, cluing you in that someone or something is powerful?

3. What are some examples that show love is more powerful than fame, force, or money?

4. In what ways is love a *choice*? What did Jesus' choices tell us about his love for us?

5. In your experience growing up, did you view love as something that had to be earned? Why or why not? Who or what shaped you in that regard?

6. John 3:16-17 says, "God so loved the world that he gave his only Son, so that everyone who believes in him won't perish but will have eternal life. God didn't send his Son into the world to judge the world, but that the world might be saved through him." What impression do these verses make upon you? Is believing them to be the truth something with which you've ever grappled in your faith? Why or why not?

7. To what extent do you believe that we, as humans, are "hard-wired" to love? Is loving something that comes naturally to us, or is it something we must be taught or must learn on our own, over time? Give reasons for your answers.

8. Look up and read Psalm 33. What evidence of God's love for us do you see in the world? Give details. What hope or comfort do you get from reading the words of this psalm? Read verses 10-11. What do you think those verses mean for us in our world today?

9. James W. Moore describes love as *beautiful*. What makes love beautiful? How is love redeeming?

10. What sets "Christlike love" apart from all other love? What did Christ teach us about forgiveness? In what

ways have you seen and experienced God's love during a difficult time or under challenging circumstances?

Activity 2: "We'll Get You Better"—Showing God's Love

[READ] The video clip about the mobile medical clinic for homeless teens mentions the word love only once, when the clinic's doctor is saying how much he loves coming to work and taking care of homeless children who need medical care. Near the end, we hear the doctor reassuring a patient, saying, "We'll get you better." Later this patient, speaking of the doctors, says, "I like them a lot, they're cool."

In lieu of *talking* to us about love, what does this video *show* us about love? Think for a moment about some of the ways love motivates you, whether it's at home, at work, at church, or elsewhere. Now think about some of the real needs you see around you in your community: Perhaps there are homeless teens where you are or homeless families. Maybe there are people who need meals, medical attention, educational opportunities, counseling, or something else that will help them thrive. As a group, use posterboard and markers to make a list of some of the specific needs you've seen in your community. Then make another list with the heading *We'll Get You Better—Showing God's Love*. Talk about and write down ideas for specific ways you can respond to these persons in need by showing them love through acts of caring and assistance, and by helping to make their lives genuinely better. Keep your focus not only on practical ways to help these persons, but also on how you can help them to feel God's love for them through your words and your caring actions.

Activity 3: "The Bible Tells Me So"

Divide the following passages of Scripture among individuals or among small teams within your larger group: Exodus 34:1-9; Psalm 33; John 1:1, 14-18; John 3:16-17; John 13:34-35; Romans 8:31-39; and 1 John 4:7-12. Ask each person or team to use their Bible to look up one of these passages and think about it or discuss it for a few minutes. Then let everyone take turns sharing with the larger group the significance or meaning of the verses they have read, focusing on what these verses say about God's love. Then (individually or in the same small teams as before) use your Bibles to locate additional Scripture passages that tell us or show us something about the nature of God's love and God's promise to love us always.

Close the Session

Focus for the Week

[READ] God's love is all-powerful, and it is a love that endures. Still, God knows that we live in a world with real pain. One of the best-known Christmas hymns, "It Came Upon the Midnight Clear" (words by Edmund H. Sears, 1849), is set to a lullaby-like melody, and its first verse speaks of heavenly angels serenading the newborn Christ Child. It paints a breathtaking picture for us of an ethereal stillness and a soul-cleansing solemnity. But the hymn's third verse, which is far less familiar to most of us, depicts a darker world. The writer, acknowledging that life is indeed hard, may as well be speaking to humankind everywhere, in any generation: "And ye, beneath life's crushing load, whose forms are bending low, / who toil along the climbing way with painful steps and slow, / look now! for glad and golden hours come swiftly on the wing. / O rest beside the weary road, and hear the angels sing!"[1]

Rulers of nations, governments, and industries rise and fall; technology can be obsolete by the time it hits the market; and tastes in music and clothes may quickly come into or go out of fashion. But God's love for us, which came down from heaven to us at Christmas in the form of a child, always has been, is now, and always will be there. Each day this week, remember this and ask God to show you deeper ways to share his love with others. Give thanks to God for the love he has for you, which nothing and no one can ever take away.

Closing Prayer

[READ] God, thank you for putting your arms around us and for enveloping us in your living love. Jesus chose the way of love. Help us to choose the way of love too, and help us to make that choice again and again, each and every day. Help us to show and to share your love with others, so that they may know you are Lord. Amen.

NOTE: Next week, Activity 2 will require items that group members will need to bring from home. **Before group members leave, ask them to bring to next week's meeting some Christmas symbol or Christmas decoration of great personal significance to them.** See the description for Activity 2 in Session 4 for further explanation of this activity.

---

1. From "It Came Upon the Midnight Clear," words by Edmund H. Sears. *The United Methodist Hymnal*, 218. In other hymnals, the stanza in question may be the hymn's fourth verse, not third. There were five stanzas in the original poem, but only four are set to music in *The United Methodist Hymnal*.

Session 4:
The Precious Memories
of Christmas

Key Scripture: Luke 2:1-20

Overview

This session examines the importance of memories and their power to touch our souls, and it shows us that Christmas memories are some of the most precious memories of all.

Learning Focus:
- realizing how Christmas reminds us that we need a Savior
- realizing how Christmas reminds us that we have a Savior
- realizing how Christmas reminds us that we can share the Savior

Prepare

As a reminder, review the sections in How to Lead This Study regarding Meeting Space and Supplies. Read pages 103 through 132 of the book *Finding Bethlehem in the Midst of Bedlam,* by James W. Moore; read over the key Scripture for this week; watch the DVD clip for Week 4 in advance; and make notes regarding topics or questions you may want to address with your group. Be sure that you have paper, pens or pencils, posterboard, markers, and Bibles, which you and your group members may need for this week's activities, as well as welcoming music if you wish.

NOTE: This week, Activity 2 involves items group members need to bring from home. **Sometime before this week's group meeting for Session 4, get in touch with all of the group members** to remind them to bring to this week's meeting some Christmas symbol or decoration of great personal significance to them. You will also need a red, green, or white cloth that you can use to create a display. See the description for Activity 2 below.

Welcome and Opening Prayer

As group members gather and greet one another, make a point to say hello to each one personally, and give everyone a few minutes to chat and to get settled. When you are ready to begin, thank everyone for coming, and remind them of the topic that you will focus on in today's meeting. Read or summarize the session Overview, and briefly highlight the points of your Learning Focus for today. Lead the group in the opening prayer printed below, or substitute your own.

Opening Prayer

[READ] Dear God, in so many ways, it's our memories that make us who we are. Help us to use our memories to grow as people and as your followers. Help us to understand memory as a gift you've given to us, to enable us to connect our past with our present and our future. And help us not to limit ourselves by our recollections of the past, but to let them guide us in ways that will help us to serve others and bring us closer to you. Amen.

Open the Session

[READ] How is your memory in general? Is it good? Not as good as it used to be? Is it something you struggle with? What types of information do you remember best? What tricks or techniques do you use to help you remember important things?

Engage

Activity 1: "The Minister's Cat" Memory Game

Invite your group members to play "The Minister's Cat," which is a Victorian-era parlor game that relies upon memory and quick-thinking ability. The following description is adapted from Wikipedia: "All players sit in a circle, and the first player describes the minister's cat with an adjective beginning with the letter *A*. (For example, "The minister's cat is an adorable cat . . .") Each player in turn then does the same, using different adjectives beginning with the same letter. Once everyone has done so, the first player begins again, describing the cat with an adjective beginning with the letter *B*. This continues for each letter of the alphabet. (In an alternate variation, the first player describes the minister's cat with an adjective beginning with the letter *A*, the second player with the letter *B*, and so on, continuing around the circle.) A player is eliminated from the game if they are unable to think of an adjective or if they repeat one previously used. Players may clap in unison or speak in a rhythmic manner during the game, setting the pace for each player to speak their line; if a player falls too far behind the pace while thinking of an adjective, he or she may also be declared eliminated" (*en.wikipedia.org/wiki/The_Minister's_Cat*).

Discuss the following questions:

1. What does this game tell you about your memory? About the importance of memory in general?
2. Why are our memories so powerful?

Read the Scripture and Discuss

Read the following Scripture passage, or ask a volunteer to read it aloud:

In those days Caesar Augustus declared that everyone throughout the empire should be enrolled in the tax lists. This first enrollment occurred when Quirinius governed Syria. Everyone went to their own cities to be enrolled. Since Joseph belonged to David's house and family line, he went up from the city of Nazareth in Galilee to David's city, called Bethlehem, in Judea. He went to be enrolled together with Mary, who was promised to him in marriage and who was pregnant. While they were there, the time came for Mary to have her baby. She gave birth to her firstborn child, a son, wrapped him snugly, and laid him in a manger, because there was no place for them in the guestroom.

Nearby shepherds were living in the fields, guarding their sheep at night. The Lord's angel stood before them, the Lord's glory shone around them, and they were terrified.

The angel said, "Don't be afraid! Look! I bring good news to you—wonderful, joyous news for all people. Your savior is born today in David's city. He is Christ the Lord. This is a sign for you: you will find a newborn baby wrapped snugly and lying in a manger." Suddenly a great assembly of the heavenly forces was with the angel praising God. They said, "Glory to God in heaven, and on earth peace among those whom he favors."

When the angels returned to heaven, the shepherds said to each other, "Let's go right now to Bethlehem and see what's happened. Let's confirm what the Lord has revealed to us." They went quickly and found Mary and Joseph, and the baby lying in the manger. When they saw this, they reported what they had been told about this child. Everyone who heard it was amazed at what the shepherds told them. Mary committed these things to memory and considered them carefully. The shepherds returned home, glorifying and praising God for all they had heard and seen. Everything happened just as they had been told. (Luke 2:1-20)

Discuss the following questions:

1. Why do we need to be reminded that we *have* a Savior or that we *need* a Savior? How is it possible that's something we could forget?

2. What do Advent and Christmas remind us about Jesus the Savior?

3. When have you relied upon a Savior to help you out of a time of darkness, brokenness, or sorrow?

4. In our times of trouble, how do our memories of what God has done before lead us away from doubt and back towards hope?

Watch the DVD clip for Week 4 entitled "The Precious Memories of Christmas."

Activity 2: Sharing Personal Christmas Memories from Home

[READ] In the video clip, we learned that one couple made their own Nativity scene in 1949 from an old lettuce crate. Today they consider it priceless. It reminds them that during a time when their family had little to nothing of any monetary value, they had everything they needed to celebrate together, to love one another, to remember Christ's birth, and to give thanks.

Share with the group something you've brought from home—a symbol, an item, or a story, for example—that you or your family use at Christmas every year. Explain why this particular thing holds great personal meaning for you. (If you've forgotten to bring an item from home, then simply try to describe it in some detail.) After every group member has had a turn, drape a red, green, or white cloth over a table, take all of the Christmas things that have been brought, and carefully arrange them together in a nice display. Take photographs of the display for your group members to remember how you've combined your personal Christmas mementos to make one more special reminder of this Christmas you are sharing together.

Questions for Group Discussion and Personal Reflection

1. In addition to anything you've already shared with the group, what are some of your personal favorite family traditions or general customs of the Christmas season? Is there one that means more to you or to your family than any other? If so, describe it.

2. James W. Moore describes memory as "absolutely crucial for our sense of personal identity" (*Finding*

Bethlehem in the Midst of Bedlam, page 104). What are your impressions of that idea? In what way is that true for you personally?

3. How can we use our memory to shape us in positive ways, rather than letting bad memories control us?

4. Does Christmas bring back mostly good memories for you? Describe one of your favorite or most vivid memories of Christmas, either a recent memory or one long past. What made this memory stay with you the way it has?

Why do we typically associate Christmas with *home*, whether it's gratitude for being at home on that special day and at that special time of year or a longing to be there if one is away?

James W. Moore talks about Charles Dickens's *A Christmas Carol*, the character of Ebenezer Scrooge, and Scrooge's story of redemption. To what degree do you believe Scrooge's conversion was due to a voluntary change of heart borne out of compassion? Is it possible Scrooge was motivated primarily or strictly by fear? Apart from whether it is effective, is fear a "good" motivator or "the right kind" of motivation to have? Give reasons for your answers.

What do we have in common with Scrooge? How is his story also our story? What does Scrooge's story show us about the need to share a Savior?

Activity 3: Leave Your Own Christmas Legacy

[READ] What are your impressions and thoughts after watching the video clip about German prisoners of war making a Nativity scene? What does this story say to you about needing and calling upon a Savior in times of great need?

We learned that the men's group in the video had adopted the German prisoners' Nativity scene and raised money for a building in which to house it and display it every year at Christmas. These efforts were described as "a labor of love" to preserve their Christmas traditions as a legacy for future generations.

Work with one another on ways your group can leave some legacy for future generations of your families, your townsfolk, or your fellow church members. This legacy could be messages of faith and love, reminders of important events in your shared history, or something else. Talk with your pastor, a longtime church member, or your town historian about what such a faith legacy might entail, or ask about ways you can help support some effort that is already underway. Keep your focus on future generations, and decide what you will want them to know and remember about Christ's love.

Close the Session

Focus for the Week

[READ] Preparing our hearts and homes this time of year for the coming of the Christ Child reminds us of God's precious gifts to us. It reminds us that we need a Savior, that we have a Savior, and that we can share a Savior. Each day this week, write down something important you want to remember about Christ and his love for you. Select something you want to carry with you through the rest of the Christmas season, into the new year and beyond, to remind yourself that God is love, and that God sent his only son, Jesus, to save us and to be a light to all the world.

Closing Prayer

[READ] Dear Lord, thank you for the joy of good Christmas memories and traditions. Help us use our memories in constructive ways to gain a clearer understanding of where we are now and where you'd like us to go. Help us to share the joy of Christ's saving love with others in ways that will "touch their hearts and warm their souls," as you have done for us. And help us to remember always that nothing can ever separate us from your love. Amen.

NOTE: Next week, for Activity 1, you will need a few small, battery-powered flashlights or penlights, and a small handheld mirror for each group member. Before they leave, ask group members to bring some of these items next week. See the description for Activity 1 in Session 5.

Session 5:
Mind the Light

Key Scriptures: John 1:1-5; Isaiah 9:6

Overview

This session looks at our responsibility as Christians to "keep the light of Christ aglow in this world."

Learning Focus:
- Our job as Christians is to mind the light of peace.
- Our job as Christians is to mind the light of hope.
- Our job as Christians is to mind the light of love.

Prepare

As a reminder, review the sections in How to Lead This Study regarding Meeting Space and Supplies. Read pages 133 through 144 of the book *Finding Bethlehem in the Midst of Bedlam*, by James W. Moore; read over the key Scriptures for this week; watch the DVD clip for Week 5 in advance; and make notes regarding topics or questions you may want to address with your group. Be sure that you have paper, pens or pencils, posterboard, markers, Scotch tape or masking tape, and Bibles, which you and your group members may need for this week's activities, and welcoming music if you wish.

NOTE: For Activity 1, you will need a few small, battery-powered penlights or flashlights, and a small handheld mirror for each group member. See the description for Activity 1, below. For Activities 2 and 3, you will need Internet access and a computer or some other device for the group to view websites together. See the descriptions for Activities 2 and 3 below.

Welcome and Opening Prayer

As group members gather and greet one another, make a point to say hello to each one personally, and give everyone a few minutes to chat and to get settled. When you are ready to begin, thank everyone for coming, and remind them of the topic you will be focusing on in today's meeting. Read or summarize the session Overview, and briefly highlight the points of your Learning Focus for today. Lead the group in the opening prayer printed below, or substitute your own.

Opening Prayer

[READ] Dear Lord, thank you for sending the Christ Child into our world to light our darkness and to show us the way to peace, hope, and love. Thank you for asking us to be your helpers in this as well. It's a very big task, and there is much at stake. Now that Christmas has come, we pray that you will lead us beyond Bethlehem and into the world, where we can be your faithful servants in shining Christ's light of peace, hope, and love for all to see and believe. These things we ask in the name of your Son, Jesus Christ. Amen.

Open the Session

[READ] Can you remember what you once learned in science class? Let's talk for just a few minutes about light: What are some of its basic characteristics and properties? How do we typically feel or respond when we need light in a darkened room or a house, but we can't find the light switch or the power is out?

Engage

Read the Scripture and Discuss

Read the following Scripture passage, or ask a volunteer to read it aloud:

In the beginning was the Word
    and the Word was with God

and the Word was God.
The Word was with God in the beginning.
Everything came into being through the Word,
    and without the Word
    nothing came into being.
What came into being
    through the Word was life,
    and the life was the light for all people.
The light shines in the darkness,
    and the darkness doesn't extinguish the light.

(John 1:1-5)

[ASK] What do these verses from John 1 say to you about Jesus the Son and his relationship with God the Father? How does the image of light breaking into the darkness as a metaphor for Christ resonate with you?

Activity 1: Reflecting the Light

Give one member of your group a battery-powered flashlight or penlight. A laser pointer will work for this activity as well, though you must take care to avoid shining it in someone's eyes. Give each of the other members a small handheld mirror. Arrange your seats in a wide circle. Make your meeting space as dark as possible, with everyone seated for safety. Ask the person with the flashlight to turn it on and shine it across the circle toward one person's mirror. Have that person then try to reflect the light back across to another person's mirror, who then directs it to someone else. Continue this exercise until everyone is reflecting light in their mirror at the same time. If this proves to be too difficult to achieve, repeat the exercise from the beginning, but this time with one or two people exchanging their mirrors for additional flashlights. Experiment also with reflecting points of light into different areas of the room. Then, turn on the main lights and discuss the following questions:

1. What did you notice about how the light behaved as it was reflected back and forth?
2. What insight from this activity can we apply to our calling as Christians to be the light of Christ in the world?
3. What challenges do we face in being the light of Christ, and what strengths do we have?

Watch the DVD clip for Week 5 entitled "Mind the Light."

Activity 2: Share the Bounty—One Family

[READ] What are your general impressions of the story we saw in the video clip about Christmas for AIDS orphans? In what ways was Purity, the young woman featured in the clip, a reflection of the light of Christ for those around her? What personal characteristics does it take to be someone like her? How are you inspired or challenged by Purity's actions, as she opened up her table to share Christmas with other orphans together as one family in God?

Take a few minutes to make a group list of some of the many things in your lives you are thankful for and would consider to be a bounty. Write them down on posterboard and circle a few of the items listed that you might consider to be the most worth sharing.

ZOE (Zimbabwe Orphans Endeavor) was founded in 2004 as a mission of the North Carolina Annual Conference of The United Methodist Church. Its mission is to help orphaned and vulnerable children help themselves by empowering them to move from extreme poverty to self-reliance in only three years.

Spend a few minutes as a group getting to know some of the children ZOE has helped, by reading their stories here: *www.zoehelps.org/meet-a-zoe-child*.

Then, spend a few more minutes together visiting ZOE's "Get Involved" page (*www.zoehelps.org/get-involved*), to learn about ways you and your group could "share the bounty" with which you've been blessed, and about the many different ways available for you to partner with ZOE to help.

Designate one or more members of your group to coordinate your efforts to be involved.

Activity 3: Thanking Our Veterans

[READ] What are your thoughts after watching the story about holiday wreaths for veterans? How can we best honor in our hearts those who have given and sacrificed so much?

There are many ways to help, both nationally and locally. Take some time together as a group to visit the following websites for more information on how you can help our veterans and their families:

www.volunteer.va.gov
www.usvetsinc.org/how-to-help
www.military.com/veterans-day/ways-to-give-back-to-veterans.html
www.cnn.com/2013/11/05/us/iyw-simple-ways-to-honor-veterans

Questions for Group Discussion and Personal Reflection

1. What are your impressions of the story of Kate Walker, the caretaker of the lighthouse (*Finding Bethlehem in the Midst of Bedlam*, pages 134–35)?

2. From your own experiences, recount a story of someone who shared the light of Christ with others. Would you consider this person ordinary or extraordinary, and why?

3. What are some of the sacrifices you believe we are called to make as Christians? Why do we sometimes overlook the idea of personal sacrifice in the daily practice of our faith? How can we keep that part of our Christian calling at the forefront of what we do?

4. What does it mean to you as a Christian to mind the light of peace, to mind the light of hope, and to mind the light of love? Where should we look for our guidance on how to do this well?

5. Achieving peace on earth seems a very tall task, indeed. How does God call us as Christians to respond to the difficulty of the job?

6. What have you learned in the course of this study about bedlam, including how to view it as a Christian and how to deal with it? What have you enjoyed most about your time of fellowship together with your group? How and where will you be celebrating the birth of the Christ Child this Christmas season?

Close the Session

Closing Reflection

[READ] As we go our separate ways, think back over all you've learned and experienced during these weeks of Advent. Remember the way James W. Moore put it: "Every now and then, we find Bethlehem . . . the real spirit, the real meaning of Christmas" that breaks through the bedlam and keeps us going (*Finding Bethlehem in the Midst of Bedlam*, page 12). This Christmas (and beyond), keep looking for those kinds of every-now-and-then moments around you. And keep looking for ways you can make those kinds of moments for someone else. Give thanks to God for the Christ Child, "Wonderful Counselor, Mighty God, Eternal Father, Prince of Peace" (Isaiah 9:6).

Closing Prayer

[**READ**] Dear God, thank you for giving us the hope we needed to wait for and to welcome the Christ Child, who is the Prince of Peace, the Savior, and the Hope of the world. In a world of busyness and bedlam, you warm our hearts and lift our souls with your everlasting love. Show us the way to go out into the world to mind the light of Christ and to share the good news of Christmas with others. These things we ask in the name of your Son, Jesus Christ, Immanuel, "God with us." Amen.